Kimberly's Special Way of Learning

What do you do when you just can't be like everyone else?

Kimberly's Special Way of Learning

Copyright © 2025 Dr. Ann Jones.

Published by IAM Harvest Network, Inc. DBA Real Talk Kim Publishing
Fayetteville, GA 30215

ISBN: 979-8-9922123-1-0
Library of Congress Control Number: 979-8-9922123-1-0

First Edition
For permissions, inquiries, or to request bulk purchases, please contact dreannjones@gmail.com

This book is lovingly dedicated to all children, parents, and educators who celebrate unique ways of learning and embrace the beauty of diversity.

Printed in the United States of America

From a proud Mimi who
loves her family!

Kimberly was so excited!
She was on her way to stardom
as a rising first grader!

She knew she could do anything
because that's what her
mommy always said!

Kimberly was a curious little girl always asking questions, but she never expected first grade to be so scary.

After the first week of first grade, Kimberly wailed in fear. She knew first grade would never be as fun as kindergarten.

She wasn't understanding anything.

Kimberly had loved kindergarten, but first grade brought all kinds of problems.

What happened to the little girl that could do anything?

While her friends seemed to understand phonics and the many sounds of the alphabet, Kimberly needed more time.

While others were moving on to the next lesson, she did not understand how first grade was so easy for her friends.

Why did her brother, Rob, always get to play with his friends after school while she worked so hard on her homework?

Kimberly admired her brother but often felt frustrated. Rob seemed to race through his schoolwork. His grades were always at the top of his class.

He was such a success and she felt like a loser.

No matter how hard she studied, she could not remember her spelling words or finish her assignments like Rob.

How could they be so different? Why could she not understand what she was trying to read?

One evening, after a tough day at school, Kimberly sat with her mom, tears welling up in her eyes.
Every day, she would spend hours studying.

The words she learned today, she could not remember tomorrow.

Kimberly's teacher, Mrs. Parker said, "Kimberly, you have a unique way of learning and that's something special.

Just because reading is easy for your friends doesn't mean that you are different.

So, let's find a way to learn that works for you."

Kimberly also worked with Mr. Thomas, the school's learning specialist, who showed her new strategies for reading.

Mrs. Parker gave her different tools to use like colorful markers to help her organize her thoughts and fun games that made math easier to understand.

Slowly, Kimberly began to see progress. One day, she raised her hand in class and confidently read the story out loud. No one knew she had spent hours rehearsing that short story so she could fit in with her class.

Her classmates clapped, and Kimberly beamed with pride.

Kimberly realized she had trouble learning, so she discovered a new way to learn!

She told her mom, "I will be successful one day, and I will not be known as the girl with a learning problem. I may not be able to learn as my friends or my brother, but I will find a way to make a difference."

By the end of the year, Kimberly realized that, with determination and the right support, she could do anything she set her mind to. She learned that being different was a strength, not a weakness.

And even though her brother still excelled in school, Kimberly felt proud of her own achievements.

She knew that her hard work and perseverance made her strong and special in her own way.

Today, Kimberly is president of several companies. She can do whatever she makes up her mind to do. She learned that just because people label you as one thing, it doesn't mean that's who you are.

Determine your outcome in life. When you make up your mind, you can become whatever you dream.

THE END

ABOUT THE AUTHOR

Dr. Ann Jones is a writer and author,
mother of daughter, Kimberly, known as
Real Talk Kim,
and son, Rob, and the grandmother of five
handsome grandsons.

www.ingramcontent.com/pod-product-compliance
Lightning Source LLC
Chambersburg PA
CBHW060815090426

42737CB00002B/69